Digging Deeper Than Before

Poems by
Misty J. Grimes

PublishAmerica
Baltimore

© 2005 by Misty J. Grimes.
All rights reserved. No part of this book may be reproduced, stored in a retrieval system or transmitted in any form or by any means without the prior written permission of the publishers, except by a reviewer who may quote brief passages in a review to be printed in a newspaper, magazine or journal.

First printing

ISBN: 1-4137-8670-7
PUBLISHED BY PUBLISHAMERICA, LLLP
www.publishamerica.com
Baltimore

Printed in the United States of America

*Dedicated to those I love
who have gone home before me.
You are truly missed.*

Irene Marie-Claire Harris
March 24, 1927 – January 13, 1991

David Hoyt Gaines
May 18, 1960 – December 18, 1996

Roy Roger Thigpen
March 7, 1945 – April 21, 2003

Acknowledgments

There are so many people who have been there for me over the years to offer their support and encouragement to me with not only my writing but with my personal growth as well. Without them none of this would be happening right now. To all of you I am truly grateful.

Kell and Melena Carpenter for your constant friendship through the years. You are both (and Kelsey) very special to me. I hope we will always be there for each other.

The whole BSU class of 1990. You know who you are and I appreciate you all.

Rick Bodwell—we've been through a lot together but have managed to remain friends. You are very special to me—always remember that.

My mother, Rita M. Sarlls. I love you, Mom, more than you'll ever know. I'm so glad that God healed our relationship. I don't know what I'd do without you.

To my stepfather, Glenn Sarlls—thanks for always being there for our family and for putting up with us over the years. It takes a special man to do what you have done and continue to do.

To Judy Thigpen for putting up with me all these years and doing your best to "straighten" me out. Thanks for being there.

To the father I didn't know until my adult years but am glad I found—Ron Willert. Thanks for all you do for me.

To all my siblings—Becky Thigpen, Sandy Medlin, Sherry Thigpen, Charlie Thigpen, Kari Robinson, Jason Willert, Peter Sarlls and Andrew Sarlls. You all mean the world to me and I thank God for each of you every day.

Dr. Lee Gillis who took this scared little girl under his wing and helped her become a confident woman. You are a very special part of my life.

David Veal. Without your support and encouragement of me and my writing, as well as my recovery, I wouldn't be here to write this today. Thank you from the bottom of my heart. May we one day meet again.

Peggy Ruhl—thanks for helping me learn to dance again. I miss our meetings at Denny's. You are the best friend anyone could ever ask for. You made my recovery possible through your support, encouragement and prayers. A simple thank you just doesn't seem to be enough. I love you.

Dr. Don Harris. Even though you may not consider me one of your success stories, you helped me more than you'll ever know. Thanks for putting up with me for three years and sticking with me even when you were ready to throw your hands up and quit. Because you never quit, neither did I. Thank you for always being there.

Dr. Otis Andrews—for helping me to see why Christ loves me just as I am. You've been there at all the turning points in my life and that means a lot to me.

Rod Callahan—for helping me to see that there is life after death. Without you I couldn't of survived the loss of my first love (David Gaines). Thanks for helping me to learn to love again. Thanks for helping me draw closer to God and seek him for my support, strength and encouragement.

Marilyn Davis—though it may not seem like it, I learned a lot from you during my eight months at North House. You are a wonderful teacher and I owe a lot in my recovery to you and your teachings. You will never be forgotten.

Most of all, to my loving husband, James T. Grimes. I waited 37 years for the right man and I'm glad God led me to you. You mean the world to me. Your support and encouragement have made all the difference in my life. Thanks for always being there for me and for putting up with me. I love you.

*Susan —
you've been a wonderful
teacher & an even better
friend. Thanks for everything.*

Digging Deeper Than Before

"A well chosen anthology is a complete dispensary of medicine for the more common mental disorders, and may be used as much for prevention as cure."

– Robert Ranke Graves, *On English Poetry*

War

Nothing ever goes the way I think it should
One minute up
The next minute down
A constant battle to regain control
Of a life forever in a tailspin
Anger
Hate
Bitterness
The enemies of war
Never defeated
Growing in strength
Gaining unseen control
Unaware of when it starts
Never knowing if it will end
One battle after another
Rages on within
Wanting to raise the white flag
Losing it time and again
As the forces within disarm me
Not letting me give in
To lay down in defeat
Would be an insult to all
They've not fought the battle
Years on end
In order to face defeat
They continue to rise
Fighting to win
Even for just one day
The small victories
Will one day be enough
To say the war was won

How I See Things

I look at life through clouded eyes
Covered with the effects of sin
Greed
Lust
Anger
Just to name a few
I look to the world to find relief
Wanting the joy it holds so deep
Sin creeps in and steals it away
It is false anyway
A fleeting, temporary solution
To an eternal need
It grows bigger by the hour
Never leaving me in peace
Searching for a way in
Finding one wall after another
Never before has it been so real
Loneliness
Sadness
Grief
All consuming what little light
Having penetrated deep within
Meeting a dismal end
In a life that needs to mend

Right or Wrong

I can't decide what to do
What is right
What is wrong
Who decides
How is something determined right
How is something determined wrong
Who writes the laws
Who enforces them
Who shows us how to change
So that we do
What is right
Rather than the wrong
So we see clearly
And know without a doubt
That the decisions we make
Are right
Or wrong
And what to do if we fall
Into a pit
Full of deceit
Clawing away at the needs
That cause us to believe
We're wrong
Or right
It's okay to proceed
Does it matter
Which way we go
Right or
Wrong
Won't it all lead

Back to fulfilling
Our selfish needs
Do we always do what's right
What's wrong
Does it matter
Don't all our decisions
Lead to one goal
Fulfilling the desires
Of a needy soul

Confusion

How do you get someone to understand
That which you don't understand yourself?
How do you respond to questions
You know there are no answers to?
How do you change your behaviors
When they all appear unchangeable?
How do you find hope
In a seemingly hopeless situation?
How do you express your thoughts
When they are a tangled web?
How do you verbalize those things
That no words can express?
Your deepest thoughts
Your darkest needs
All lurk on the edge of sanity
Wanting to find freedom
In expression
Of the inexpressible
Find meaning
In the meaningless
And make it all make sense.

Please God, Not Tonight

She sits alone in the corner
Longing for a gentle touch
When out of the darkness he appears
And says, "I love you very much."

His love fills her with hate and fear
For what he does is not right
Yet here he is once again
And she prays, "Please God, not tonight."

But tonight is like last night
And every night before
When the lips that say "I love you"
Probe and invade once more.

Every night it's something new
And only he knows what lies ahead
In her fear she prays, "Please God, not tonight"
As gently he places her on the bed.

Tonight it's more than she can bear
So she escapes to a world all her own
Where pain and lust no longer exist
A place where only true love is shown.

Afterward he leaves without a word
She longs inside for someone to help her fight
Through her tears she silently cries,
"Please God, let it be tonight."

In the Darkness of the Night

In the darkness of the night
The ghosts come out of hiding
No longer afraid of being seen
They are quick to make their presence known.

In the darkness of the night
Security slips quickly away
The light of day is no longer a safe haven
Vanishing with the twinkling of the first star.

In the darkness of the night
Apparitions of the mind become real
Making themselves right at home
Leaving no place to run.

In the darkness of the night
Time appears to stand still
The moon glows bright as the sun
Offering none of its warmth.

In the darkness of the night
You wait anxiously for the dawn
Knowing with the light of day
The monsters will once again be gone.

Who Are They?

They hide in the corners
Drawing attention to themselves
They stand in the middle of chaos
Being ignored as the world goes rushing by

They sit in the dark
Hoping to be lost
They come out into the light
And fade into the background.

They see all and know all
Everything is but a fading mist
They hope and they pray
As it all slops slowly away.

They are all an unsolved mystery
Whims and desires that disappear
They are a thousand piece puzzle
No one can put together.

They run the race
Losing ground each day
They are the rain that falls
Drowning and destroying it all.

Madness

There is a method to this madness
Though I don't know what it is
When one day I'm up
And the next I'm down
Or when I don't know
From one minute to the next
If things will be calm
Or raging like a mighty, rushing wind
What causes this madness to stir?
What causes it to slip away?
Do I have control over any of it
Or is it up to the gods of love and war?
All these things I may never know
But one thing is forever sure
The madness will always be near
And through it all I will endure.

Guess If You Can

It comes like the dawn when you're fast asleep
It comes like the night when you just can't sleep
It comes in quick like the afternoon tide
It leaves as slowly as the bluebird flies
It invades like a winter storm
It lingers like a long hot summer
It disappears like the moon behind the clouds
It is as vast as the midnight sky
It always takes prisoners like war
It often rushes like the ocean waves
It is a destructive as hurricane winds
It is as calm as a fall day
It is as loud as the roaring thunder
It is as quiet as a mouse
It is as mysterious as the universe
It is as hungry as a shark in the sea
Guess if you can
And let me see
What it is that lies
Deep inside of me

Shadows of Yesterday

Nothing makes sense anymore
The voices keep screaming in my head
Everyone wants something different
None of it anything good
Just different ways of escaping
The things that haunt us most
The shadows of yesterday
The demons of today
All combine to wreak havoc
STOP!!!!!
Please make it stop
Tell him to stop screaming
Her to stop crying
Being scared
Lonely
Confused
Hurt
A flood of emotions none are sure of
All fear what is to come
Rage
Tears
Death
The fear of the unknown
The unrest is unsettling
Causing panic

The Darkness I

I sit in the darkness
Sleep a fleeting luxury
Chased away by yesterday's ghosts
And tomorrow's fears

The darkness calls to me
An unwilling participant
Struggling to find the light
Lying in silent surrender.

I reach out to claim the dark
Thick and unyielding
Playing its games
No one rising victorious

It claims me without warning
Cold and unforgiving
Bringing the ghosts of yesterday
To steal the joy from today.

An ever present reminder
Of days best forgotten
Offering no escape
Adding more misery

The darkness offers no escape
Chains holding fast
Turning a deaf ear
To the screams of one tormented

Pride

Memories pasted on the wall
Reminders of days gone by
Much was lost
In foolish pride

We think we gain the world
Yet we forfeit our soul
Following undauntingly folly
Then lie down to die

Never ceasing in our pursuit
To catch each fleeting whim
With no regard for the cost
Blind to all that is lost

Snatching reality out of life's grasp
While we trudge headlong
Along the dark and lonely path
We've created all our own

Strangers on a journey
Constructed of our own demise
Alone along the darkened paths
We walk aimlessly and unaware

It is over before it has begun
Never more to roam
Looking up at the wall of life
Seeing that it's gone

The Prisoners

Alone in a world that seems so cruel
Surrounded by a fortress of fear
Entrapped in a tomb of shame
Carefully holding captive every tear

All the prisoners locked safely away
Eagerly search for a way to escape
Wanting so much to be set free
Yet all remaining to participate in the masquerade

Occasionally one will get beyond the wall
And enjoy the small taste of freedom it receives
But soon the guard invades the joy
No longer allowing the captive to feel relieved

Daily the captives look for small glimpses of hope
Something that will show them their days of bondage are drawing to a close
Daily they are disappointed
For a guard waits at the prison wall ready to defend

The prisoners smile with joy and anticipation
As they see one guard slowly fade away
Their hopes are soon diminished
As another guard rises to block their way

How long will their pleas to the keeper go unheard?
How long will their cries for freedom be refused?
Are captives what they are destined to always be?
Or will the keeper one day listen and bring an end to their years of misery?

The Ocean and Me

I stand upon the shore and watch the waves crash upon the beach
I know how the ocean feels for my emotions crash within me
I think about all the different life forms that live deep within the ocean
I have life forms deep within me—
emotions that swim around aimlessly
As the ocean is not easily understood, neither are my emotions
The ocean stares at me dark and mysterious,
yearning to be explored
Each new emotion brings with it feelings of mystery and confusion, a need to be explored
Like explorers who fear remaining in the ocean too long because of sharks
I fear what I will find if I explore the depths of who I am too long
The ocean calms and is again peaceful
Inside of me things are always like the crashing waves
As the tide rises and retreats each day
So do the emotions that make me who I am

The Darkness II

Hiding in the darkness
Far away from prying eyes
Afraid to let the people see
The reason the child cries

Alone in the darkness
Is where the child stays
For if others caught a glimpse of her
They would know where the real she lays

Staying in hiding is her goal
She feels it is better to remain unknown
For seeing eyes bring more pain
At least from what she's been shown

Is alone in the darkness
Where she'll always stay?
Or will the light come
To show her another way?

Until she will come out to search
For answers not yet known
She will never know what lies outside
The world she's created of her own

The Hands

I stood in the hallway looking up at your face
The smile there showed of love and care
Yet your hands told me something different
As did your words—"Don't tell, you wouldn't dare."

So deep inside our secret was locked away
Each smile and touch reminded me
That love and care did not go with the hands
But a twisted sort of love that I had failed to see

Soon I forgot the smiles and touches
Until other hands came to invade again
The door was opened and twisted love returned
In the hands of another determined to sin

This time the hands were discovered by another
And I was blamed for letting them invade
Twisted love once again claimed my life
Causing me to be part of a masquerade

Years later I still feel the hands
Wanting to claim a life in repair
But a strength deep within lets me know
My life will not forever be in despair

The hands that showed me twisted love are gone
Never again will they silence this child
For I know that true love can abide
In the mending soul of a wounded child

A Letter to All

I am supposed to love you
But I don't have to like you
How can that be?
For to love someone
Means you like some part of them
Yet hate for you
Is all that fills me
Anger burns within
At the mention of your name
Love is the last
Thing on my mind
Much less any liking
My stomach turns
At the sight of you
I wish I could
Strike out at you
To release the storm
That rages within
Yet I leave it locked inside
To hurt myself again and again
The question of why runs
Always through my mind
If I was ever loved
Or even liked to the smallest degree
Why did you hurt me?
Why do you hurt those you love?
Why are conditions placed on acceptance?
Why can't you accept me for me
And love me just as I am?
I long to be liked,

Accepted
And loved
Yet it appears this will never be
Maybe if I could forgive
All these things I long for
Will be allowed to come in
Maybe they are already there
Hidden by the anger
Hurt and Hate
That have control over me
What will it take
For the veil to be lifted
So I will be able to say
I like what I see
For it is all a part of me

The Child Within

The pictures tell of days gone by
When hopes and dreams were still young
The eyes of the young child show happiness
But no one can see the terror that hides inside

As years go by the pictures change
Hopes and dreams have faded away
The happiness that once danced in her eyes
Is replaced by a sadness no one but she can explain

What secrets does she keep that make her look so sad?
What terrors lie deep inside that no one else can see?
Are the hopes and dreams forever replaced by fear and pain?
Or will the happiness and joy return again someday?

Who will be the one to touch her life and take away the fear?
Who will be the one to help her release the joyful child that lies within?
Who will be the one to renew the hopes and dreams she once held so dear?

The answers to all these questions lie deep within her
For she is the only one who knows what's needed to renew her sense of hope
She must be willing to reach out and trust the one person who can help her see
The child who was once full of hopes and dreams is still waiting within

Once Again the Darkness Comes

I sit in the darkness
Sleep a fleeting luxury
Chased away by yesterday's ghosts
And tomorrow's fears

The darkness calls to me
An unwilling participant
Struggling to find the light
Lying in silent surrender

I reach out to claim the dark
Thick and unyielding
Playing its games
No one rising victorious

It claims me without warning
Cold and unforgiving
Bringing the ghosts of yesterday
To steal the joy from today

An ever present reminder
Of days best forgotten
Offering no escape
Adding more misery

The darkness offers no escape
Chains holding fast
Turning a deaf ear
To the screams of one tormented

Goodbye

I want to resign and leave it all behind
Let someone else take the wheel
I've driven this road long enough
And can go not one more mile

Relief will never come as long as I'm here
Only when I'm laid to rest
When the memories that haunt me
And fears that taunt me
All close their eyes in death

Only then will I know the peace I desire
Only then will I see beyond my doubts
For only in my solemn slumber
Will the ghosts that haunt me finally disappear

There is no good in this life I lead
Only emptiness and strife
I have fought the fight the best I could
Yet victory is not mine to have
I will win only when I lie down to sleep

Misery is my only friend
Fear its dark companion
Together they have beaten me down
Till I have nothing else to give
So I will surrender and never live again

I'm tired of the battles
And want only to rest
Death opens its arms to me
Beckoning me to come in
Embracing me with its cold kiss

No one knows just how it feels
To live the life I lead
If they knew they'd surely see
That surrender is all there is for me
And they'd release me to that which I seek

There is no fear in the darkness
It left a long time ago
Taking a life that was never lived
Without a moment of regret
I lay down in peaceful rest

It is no great loss to me
I've taken much and given little
No one could say I didn't try
Strength and courage were mine for a time
They'll go with me to a better place

I leave with no words of comfort
Knowing you'll find it in yourself
To forgive the one who could only see
Happiness in her death

Remembering

It hurts too much to think of yesteryear
And for all of them I shed a tear

I want to leave the past behind
And put it forever out of my mind

But in order to do that I must recall
I must relive them one and all

Doing this I know will hurt
But with these thoughts I can no longer flirt

The memories have been locked away
And there I wish they'd forever stay

But the time has come when I must let go
I need to let the memories flow

For only through this can I be sure
That my life won't be forever a blur

Anywhere but Here

Anywhere would be better than here
For being here is a scary place
It is a place where little goes right
And a smile rarely crosses a face

There is nothing but darkness here
With voices always yelling and screaming
Never knowing what to say or do
But watch each wound slowly bleeding

If the light appears run and hide
Don't let them see what lies inside
Maybe they want to help heal the hurt
To do what no one else ever tried

The help offered is scary too
Unsure if it is what is wanted
Knowing it is what is needed
Yet always hesitating to get started

Internal War

Trapped inside a hostile world
Trying to find a way out
Searching for the path to freedom
Continually weighed down by doubt

In the private world of her own
Many battles are being fought
Wars that are to help her grow
Go against all that she's been taught

The soldiers try to tell her
They come to bring her peace
For she is now a captive
Searching for the day of her release

The soldiers that try to help her
Make her cringe in fear
For they represent things she'd rather forget
Things she does not hold very dear

She grows weary from the fighting
And digs down deep for strength
Hoping beyond all hope
That she'll have what it takes

She knows the day will come
When she'll be able to give in
Letting the soldiers wage the war
That will restore her once again

Silence

Looking deep into your eyes
I see the pain you bear
Within my heart a feeling stirs
Wanting to show you how much I care

Words cannot always express
All that we feel inside
The silence becomes a stumbling block
Where unspoken feelings forever abide

Yet in the silence a bond is made
Two hearts come together in a warm embrace
Finding comfort and escape
In a very wonderful place

The Volcano

A volcano looks beautiful on the outside
Peaceful sitting in the valley
But no one knows what lies deep inside
Daily it builds and builds, rising ever closer to the top
Finally the pressure builds so much it can
No longer remain within
As it seeps over the sides,
The volcano loses it once beautiful appearance
Slowly more and more pours out, burning hot
Those closest to the volcano are hurt by the eruption
They fail to understand how something so beautiful
Could eject something so ugly and hurtful
After several days the volcano is once again quiet
The beauty and peacefulness returns
People close to the volcano once again enjoy its beauty
They wonder what made it so ugly
And if it will ever happen again
They decide to enjoy the beauty of it
And forget it was at one time ugly

Young Love

I remember the day we met as if it were yesterday;
For it was the day you captured my heart.
The warmth of your blue eyes touched the depths of my soul;
The love in your smile filled my emptiness.
My love for you is no longer a secret,
I expressed my feelings the best I could and was sure I would feel the same way too.
But my dreams were cruelly crushed by words that tore at my heart.
My world seemed to fall apart, for the bright spot of it no longer was.
How could a love so fresh and young, shrivel and die before it had a chance to live and grow?
It seems unfair that a love so strong should go unnourished and never develop into what it could have been.
The cold and the emptiness have now returned to fill the place in my heart my love for you once filled.
But deep within a spark of hope remains, waiting for the day when you will once again fill the emptiness within.

Teach Me to Accept Love

My heart cries out to you
With a deep and painful hurt
Faces flash through my mind
Of those I have loved and lost.
I love you, that is true
But I reject the love you try to return
For I fear I will lose you too.
Yet how can that be
When you have promised one great thing,
That you will never leave me nor forsake me.
I don't want your love
Yet my soul yearns for a love that only you can provide
Teach me to accept the love you so freely give
A love that will uplift and sustain me;
A love that will fill the holes of my shattered heart;
A love that will forever be true;
A love that will never let go

I Wonder

All has gone black
All is spinning round and round
When will this whirlwind stop
When will it all calm down?

Everything is but a question
Everything adds up to a lot of pain
Will the answers ever come
Will there be someone else to blame?

There is a hole of emptiness
There is crying deep within
Is there a special someone
Is there a new place to begin?

Untitled

The anger burns inside of me
Searching for a way out
But I push it back, deeper and deeper
Because in my self there is doubt…
Doubt that once it is finally released
I will no longer maintain control…
Control of the defenses I have built
To protect this fragile thing called a soul.
Eventually a hole will be burned through the wall
And the anger will seep through once again
To touch every part of my troubled soul
Waiting to see if I will begin…
Begin to deal with the fire that consumes,
And takes over all that I am
But yet once again I fail,
For dealing with it I no longer can.

Questions

How do you cure internal pain,
When pain tears at every part of your soul?

How do you keep the tears from flowing,
When a river of tears is all that exists?

How do you stop the feelings of emptiness,
When empty is the only thing known?

How do you rid a mind of confusion,
When confusion is the controller of all?

How do you stop the feelings of insanity
When insanity seems the only true escape?

The Choice Is Yours

Piece after piece of a heart falls away
As each new loss tears at the soul
Slowly the life once full of joy
Empties to become a black hole.

Will emptiness remain a part
Of a heart that longs to be whole?
Or will the soul slowly release the hope
That remains chained deep within?

The chains that bind consist of anger and bitterness
While the hope that releases consists of peace and joy.

The choice is yours, which will it be…
Imprisonment of anger and eternal emptiness,
Or release of peace and eternal joy?

The choice is yours, what will it be…
A soul imprisoned forever in chains of bitterness,
Or a heart made whole by love set free?

The choice is yours, make it today…
For with each passing day you add a new chain,
And another drop of hope falls quickly away.

Winter of Discontent

Darkness covers me like a blanket
Keeping the chill of fear inside
Creating a world full of illusions
The only solution to a heart's demise.

Reality slowly creeps away like high tide
Leaving fragments of life behind
Talking with it the peace once known
Letting pain be the one to remind.

Glimpses of how life could be so good
Are chased away by the soldiers of hard times
The battlefield is littered with the corpses of joy
As new enemies arise shouting their battle cries.

Will this forever be my winter of discontent?
Will the darkness break forth into light?
Will the soldiers of good fortune arise victorious
And forever vanquish this cold, dark night?

The Betrayers

Those eyes
That smile
The cold hard stare

Those hands
That touch
The secrets were born

Those moments
That fear
The loss of innocence

Those needs
That want
The perversion of love

Those tears
That heart
The brokenness appears

Those memories
That sadness
The child remembers

Those halls
That room
The violator appears

Those dreams
That face
The recurring demands

Those hurts
That anger
The secret is out

No Direction

I come to the crossroads of life
And wonder which way I should go
For no matter which direction I turn
A roadblock prevents further travel

I come to the highway of life
And wonder which lane I should travel
For no matter which lane I choose
Road construction keeps me from proceeding

I come to find a life with no direction
And wonder why I can't find my way
For no matter how hard I try
A wall is all I see

I come to wonder what it will take
And just how long it will be
Yet I believe the answers are beyond the wall
I have built between the Lord and me

I come to know what I must do
And a deep fear fills my soul
I know perfect love casts out all fear
And down on my knees is where I belong

I come to find myself before the Lord
And wonder if he still cares
His love is forever and ever
And with me is where he will always be

The Search

A heart broken in many pieces
Lies within an empty soul
The heart in need of mending
The soul in search of a home
A mind begins to wonder if wholeness will be obtained
Years go by and the emptiness remains
All attempts to fill the holes prove meaningless
Hope quickly begins to fade
Finally the day arrives when true healing can take place
The process is slow and painful
One that is worth the wait
For now a broken heart is mended
And a lost soul has found a home
The emptiness that once consumed a life,
Is now but a memory

Secret Lover

I sit all day waiting for a glimpse of you
My heart races once I do
I wait to see if you'll come closer
And sigh deeply as you go the other way

I wait in anticipation for your visit
To hear the words that melt my private parts
Causing a stirring deep within
Bringing to life all of me

I wait longingly for your innocent touch
As it lingers a little longer than it should
Saying more than the unspoken words
Igniting a passion like no other

Is it enticing because it's forbidden
Or because it fills us with desire
Desires long dead in each of us
Longing to be fulfilled once again?

Together the voids will be filled
The darkness will float away
Leaving behind the fire of passion
And the promise of true love

I Long for the Day

I long for the days
When the sound of your voice
Brought peace and comfort
To my pain-filled soul

How I long for the days
When the gentle warmth of your embrace
Brought strength and love
To my shattered heart

How I long for the days
When walking and talking with you
Brought care and understanding
To an always confused mind

How I long for the day
When I will see you again
In a place where time will never end
And we will never say goodbye

A Specialness Created for Two

I heard our song yesterday
And the words of it pierced my heart
I closed my eyes and you were there
I opened them and you were gone.

Our lives have gone in different directions
Yours to happiness and love with another
Mine to pain and emptiness
Where did I go wrong?

You never told me you loved me
I told you many times
We shared a special part of ourselves
Yet it meant something different to you

How could something so right
Turn out to be so wrong?
Why was love denied
To a girl in need of someone to call her own?

Now that you've found someone new
I wonder where I stand
Do you still feel the specialness we shared?
The specialness that tears me in two

Am I just a voice from the past
Someone never to be thought about again
Do the times we shared
Ever cross your mind?

Whether or not I am forgotten
You will be forever remembered
For you touched my life like no other
And the specialness created for two remains locked within me

Love I Long For

When I think of you a smile crosses my face
My heart flutters deep within
As the desire for love appears once again

Locked deep inside a once troubled soul
Love is freed and allowed to roam
For it does believe it's found a home

Your eyes, your smile, your warm embrace
Bring sunshine to even the cloudiest day
And tell me more than words can say

I desire nothing more than your love
To spend the rest of my life in your arms
Enjoying each day your wit and your charm

Yet sharing a love with you is forbidden
For at night you go home to another
So my feelings, one and all, I must smother

Once again true love is denied
Love in secret is all I can find
And these emotions I must once again bind

Maybe one day it will all fall into place
And in your heart there will be a space
Where I can be, forever in your embrace

Two Loves

My heart is filled with two kinds of love
One old, one new
Both strong
The latter for you

One stems from loyalty
The other from desire
It really doesn't matter
For neither will aspire

One is forbidden
The other denied
Which way do you turn
When both forever remind?

One will soon end
The other hasn't begun
Will both end in tears
Or will one become fun?

You and me
Me and him
Which will it be
When I am ready to try again?

With You

You've seen me laugh
You've seen me cry
You've seen me broken
You've seen me whole

With you I am free
To laugh
To love
To play

With you I learn
About me
About life
About love

With you I hide
How I feel
How I hope
How I pray

With you is where I long to be
Safe in your arms
Touched by your lips
Secure in your love

I Think

I think of you
I think of me
I see us together
I want this to be

I think of love
I think of forever
I see you leave
I want that never

I think of goodbye
I think of today
I see us apart
I want you to stay

I think of emptiness
I think of now
I see nothing
I cry deep down

I think of pain
I think of my heart
I see it in pieces
I cry for each part

I think of tomorrow
I think of new love
I see me with no one
I cry for lost love

One Kiss

I'd give anything for just one kiss
To feel his soft, warm lips on mine
To feel the passion as our lips entwine
Letting nature take its course

I'd give anything for just one kiss
To feel my body respond to his
To feel his strong arms about me
Letting the spark erupt into a flame

I'd give anything for just one kiss
To feel the secret desire fade away
To feel at last what I've only dreamed of
Letting the fantasies of years come to pass

Wait for Love

I awoke this morning and thought of you
As the birds sang, their music reminded me of yours
For theirs is full of the peace and joy that lies in you
As I listen, I close my eyes and remember the warmth of your embrace
I feel the strength of the shoulder on which I once cried
As I open my eyes they fill with tears,
Is what we had lost—gone forever?
Will the arms that once held me, hold me again?
Will I again feel the warmth and strength that made me so secure?
My heart fills with the doubt and fear that ours will never be.
But in the midst of it all, a spark of hope remains
Knowing that good things come to them that wait
So wait I must, and wait I will
For a love like ours is worth waiting for

Passion

I see us entwined in a passionate embrace
The sweat glistening off our naked bodies
A silent moan escapes my lips
And I lose all control.

Feeling your body next to mine
Causes a stirring deep within
My whole body aches to have you within
Like I've never wanted anyone before

We come together in a perfect fit
Clinging together breathlessly
The feel of your hands touching my skin
Brings me to the point of ecstasy

Your lips bring to life long dead places
For the very first time I feel alive
Feeling things I never felt before
Never wanting the moment to end

I see all this in my mind's eye
And feel it all deep within
Knowing that soon the day will come
When I will have to dream no more

The Man Who Asked the Right Questions

He asked me only two questions
But they were the right ones
My heart grew to love him
Because he was sincere
My love he did not return
He couldn't. It belonged to another
One that was there before me
I told him how I felt
He responded with care. He had to.
If he were to reveal his heart
It would mean the end. For one.
A new beginning for another.
I care more than I should
But he cared when it mattered.
A heart can't forget that
No matter how hard it tries.
He is a stranger to me
I see only one side
It's enough for my heart to love
May these feelings never die
When he smiles, my heart melts
When he speaks, my soul shakes
He leaves no part unaffected
His mere presence causing my insides to stir
Never has it been so strong
Nor so wrong
Can I help it if I love
The man who asked the right questions?
Can love grow from so simple a thing
Or remain strong when he is gone?

What about the other love
That he gives willingly?
Is he happy?
Does he care?
How often does he think of me
And wish that I were there?
For me it's every day
A longing to be by his side
Just to hear his voice
Feel his touch
And sigh deep inside
It is torture to love one so elusive
To be torn apart from within
Whenever he departs
Wondering if each time will be the last
Or the beginning
Of something more
Of the one thing you desire most
To be loved
To be needed
By the man who asked the right questions

Christ's Love

When the weight of the world has got me down
I put on a smile instead of a frown

When from this world I wish to escape
It's in You I find my everlasting resting place

Each test and trial I must endure
Just proves to me Your love is sure

The arms of strength in which I long to be held
Are outstretched for me to be forever endwelled

When I survey the cross on which you died
I can see and feel the tears You cried

There are many tears I long to shed
And I know for each and every one You bled

May I always remember that when You died
I was one of the children on Your mind

A New Light

The pain you feel, I feel too
I want you to know I bear it with you

Sometimes you feel you're all alone
In this world of pain you call your own

But this burden you carry inside your heart
Is also in me, a very big part

I want you to know that I do care
And your pain and burden I do share

But together we can overcome it all
If we will just listen for Jesus' call

He is there to lend a hand
And give us the strength to take a stand

Because only through Him will the darkness fade
And a new light of hope in us is made

Wings of a Dove

The road I see
In front of me
Seems to never end
The hurdles come
One by one
And bring the pain again

Oh Lord if I had
The wings of a dove
I would fly away
To my home that waits above
But Lord I know
The wings of the dove
That I so long to have
Are here in Your arms of love

The darkness I see
Starts to fade
As the one true light
Begins to break through
Reaching deep inside
To take away the hurt

Oh Lord if I had
The wings of a dove
I would fly away
To my home that waits above
But Lord I know
The wings of the dove
That I so long to have
Are here in Your arms of love

Now I stand
In love's pure light
Filled with peace
For by your side
Is where I stand
Ready to begin again

And Lord I know
The wings of the dove
That I so long to have
I find in Your arms of love

My Lord Cried

As the rain began to fall
I looked toward the sky
For a brief moment I wondered,
What had made my Lord cry?

"Rain is rain," my friend said
But then I wondered why
If it rains when the sun shines
What makes my Lord cry?

I pondered this question
And as hard as I tried
I couldn't help but wonder
Could I be the reason my Lord cried?

When I began to examine my life
All I could do was sigh
For I soon discovered
I was indeed the reason my Lord cried.

My head hung in shame
My own shed tears I did not dry
For I had to know the reason
I made my Lord cry.

Humbly I bowed before my Lord
Knowing it was for me He died
He helped me to make the changes I needed
Because it was me who made my Lord cried.

The next day I looked up
To a clear blue sky
I smiled when I realized
My Lord no longer cries.

One True Love

As I sit here all alone
The loneliness begins to creep in
It reaches deep inside
Tugging at my heart once again.

I search and search to no avail
Looking for that one special man
Who will take all the loneliness away
Like no one else ever can.

But the longer I search
The more I can see
That no mere human
Will take the loneliness from me.

The special love for which I long
Was given to me on a cross
For it was there that He gave His life
And to Him it was no great loss.

For each and every tear
That ran down His pain-streaked face
Was shed out of love
For an undeserving race.

And with compassion in His eyes
I was on His mind
He was giving His life for me
And proving His love for all to see.

So next time I feel all alone
I've but to look to Calvary's hill
Remembering it is with His great love
That the loneliness in my heart is forever filled.

Spiritual War

Broken and shattered
I come before you
Lonely and hurting
Unsure of what to do
I've been running so long
I'm weary and worn
Ashamed to stand
Before the one I adore
I'm a victim
Of a spiritual war
I chose to give in
And not stand for my Lord
But now I've come home
Where I know I belong
No longer a victim
Of this spiritual war
In that still small voice
I hear you whisper my name
Not quite yet willing
My head hangs in shame
Then your love reached down
And took away my fears
I look up at you
And I see your tears
I'm a victim
Of a spiritual war
I chose to give in
And not stand for my Lord
But now I've come home
Where I know I belong

No longer a victim
Of this spiritual war
No longer afraid
I fall before you
Now on my knees
You show me what to do
No longer a victim
Of this spiritual war
I came just once
And you opened the door
Giving me strength
To win this war

Nothing Can Separate Us

The emptiness and hurt feels eternal
And the tears will not cease falling
Where can I find rest for my weary soul?
Where can I find healing for my crushed spirit?
I am worn, battered and bruised
From my endless pursuit of joy, happiness and love
I search and search but never find what satisfied
I struggle night and day to find the answers
And cry myself to sleep at night because I find none
Help me to see that all the answers I need are found in you
That my search is futile if I don't have you for a guide
Lavish upon me all that you have in store
Hold me in your arms as I weather these storms
Keep me safe and help me to know
That you are my daddy, I am your daughter
And that together we make a team
That nothing, nor anyone, can destroy.

True Peace

The mistakes I've made are many
The need for forgiveness is great
I seek to come before him
In need of his amazing grace

Just like Paul, I do not understand
Why I do the things I shouldn't
And run from that which I need to do
Searching for answers in everyone but you

Your love it amazes me
It is the opposite of what I know
Yet exactly what I need the most
To break the chains that bind me

I am a prisoner of this world
A captive to my sinful nature
Seeking to be filled with your spirit
And becoming a new creation

If I but wait on you
My strength will be renewed
Yet I grow weary and impatient
Settling for the easy rather than the right

In your word lies the answers
To all the questions I create
I fail to open the book to see
How my life can be brand new

As long as I choose to do it my way
I will wander lost and alone
Never knowing the true peace that comes
From simply trusting you.

Surrender

Inside there's nothing but fragments
Pieces of a tormented being
Left to fend for themselves
With no effective weapons

The battles have waged for an eternity
With few cease fires in between
No sooner do they breath a sigh of relief
Than the next one begins

Never able to see the victories
Only the wars still left to fight
Hoping the next will be the last
Always feeling as if it's the first

There is no victory in their eyes
Only failures and more struggles
Resisting the urge to wave the white flag
And finally lay down in defeat

Would surrender mean defeat?
Or would it be the means to an end?
An end to the trial and tribulation
That is their never-ending cycle?

Should they surrender to a higher power
And let him take control?
Believing the unknown in doing so
Would outweigh the cost of defeat

Turn a Page in My Life

I think of all the days gone by
And the time that went to waste
I wonder if things had been different then
Would so much have been done in haste

Days go by in what seems like years
And I wonder how my life has changed
Am I still living with the past
While Christ longs to turn another page?

Turn a page in my life, Lord
It's time for a brand new start
Let my life reflect the work you have done
Come and mend my broken heart
Let me see that the days gone by
Built a road that leads to you
And all the things I did in haste
Will work out for my good.

Burning the bridges that lead to yesterday
Cause my heart to fill with pain
Sometimes it seems easier to cross them
Than to forever remain bound in chains

One by one the bridges come down
Leaving me feeling empty and alone
The new that has replaced the old
Is hard to accept because it is unknown

Turn a page in my life, Lord
It's time for a brand new start
Let my life reflect the work you have done
Come and mend my broken heart
Let me see that the days gone by
Built a road that leads to you
And all the things that I did in haste
Will work out for my good

Daily your grace pours over me
Washing away the days of old
You fill me with new life, Lord
As you work to make me whole

All that I long to be
Is what you created me to be
Help me to be able to look at me
And see all that you see

Turn a page in my life, Lord
It's time for a brand new start
Let my life reflect the work You have done
Come and mend my broken heart
Let me see that the days gone by
Built a road that leads to You
And all the things I did in haste
Will work out for my good

Greater Is He

The question Job asked I ask too,
"Why is light given to him who suffers,
And life to the bitter of soul;
Who long for death, but there is none?"

The answer can be found in the words of the Psalmist,
"Precious in the sight of the Lord
Is the death of one of his saints."

Death is a reward for those who believe
Not a way of escape for the weary in soul
So, if death is not the answer for this wounded soldier,
Why is the desire to end this war grow stronger every day?

The author of Chronicles says,
"Do not be afraid or discouraged because of this vast army.
For the battle is not yours, but God's."

How do you let an unseen force
Fight a battle that has been solely your own;
How do you let a new commander take control
When past commanders have betrayed you?

"Though my mother and father forsake me,
The Lord will never leave me"
Is the reply the Psalmist gives.
Yet still I struggle to surrender the war

What will the outcome of this struggle be?
"Greater is He that is in me
Than he that is in the world."

(Job 3:20-21; Psalm 116:15; 2 Chronicles 20:15;
Psalm 27:10; I John 4:4)

The Never-ending Journey

Where will this road I travel lead
A road where I encounter one pothole after another
A road that is always under construction
Yet never in repair

I wander down this road aimlessly
Always searching and in need of direction
Always going the wrong way
Coming time and time again to another dead end

Traveling alone longing for another
Someone who knows the road and can help
Someone whose been there and understands
Wondering continuously if that person is there

Daily I cry, "Oh, that I had the wings of a dove,
I would fly away and be at rest—
I would hurry to my place of shelter
Far from the tempest and storm."

Then God whispers in my ear,
"Be still and know that I am God."
Being still is hard to do
When the journey seems to never end

Yet again the Lord comes to remind me
That this road I travel now
He once traveled too
It is a road He wishes to travel with me

We begin our journey with this promise,
"No temptation has seized you
Except what is common to man,
And God is faithful,
He will not let you be tempted
Beyond what you can bear
But when you are tempted
He will also provide a way out
So that you can stand up under it."

(Psalms 55:6,8; Psalm 46:10; I Corinthians 10:13)

I'll Be Your Shelter

Looking out the window
The rain begins to fall
In the midst of the storm
I wonder if You're there at all
That's when you come to me
And whisper my name
From this moment on
Things won't ever be the same
For a promise to me
Is what you have made

I'll be your shelter
In the midst of the storm
I'll cover you with
A warm embrace and
Never let you go
I'll be your shelter
When you're weary and worn
I'll be your shelter
In the midst of the storm

Feeling this storm
Still raging within
I fall on my knees
In search once again
That's when Your love shines through
And speaks to my heart
From this moment on
I know we'll never part
For a promise to me
Is what You have made

I'll be your shelter
In the midst of the storm
I'll cover you with
A warm embrace and
Never let you go
I'll be your shelter
When you're weary and worn
I'll be your shelter
In the midst of the storm

So when the storm is raging
I'll put my trust in you
For with you by my side
Is the only way
To survive the storms
That so often break through

Love I Need

My soul yearns for a love
Like none I've every known
One that reaches deep inside
And takes the emptiness away
But as long as I continue to search
This broken and fallen world
I'll never find a love
To meet my deepest needs

So I'll look to you, Lord
To find the love I so need
For you're the only one I can see
Who'll reach down to me
And give me the love
That will remain eternally

Conditional love was always given to me
But my heart longed to be
Forever free within me
For those conditions brought pain
That tore at my heart
And confused the lover in me
I learned very quickly
That is all the world could give

So I'll look to you, Lord
To find the love I so need
For you're the only one I can see
Who'll reach down to me
And give me the love
That will remain eternally

So come to me, Lord
And fill up my heart
Take away all the emptiness
This loneliness and strife
Help me to see that
Lonely isn't what I have to be
For you will fill every part

A Longing

I look at your picture
And realize
It is all I have
To remind me
Of the love I shared
With you
Yes, I still remember
The nights I was held
In your arms
I still feel your
Warm kisses
And remember
Our passionate
Nights
Please return to me
My love
I am lost
Without you
Being apart
Has broken
My heart
I want you back
By my side
Where you belong

Without You

I am lost without you
By my side
I wish we had never
Parted
The future is so
Uncertain
It scares me to think
Of me
Without you
Will we ever be
Together again?
Can our love conquer
Time and distance
Or will we move on
And find
New loves
And forget what
We had
When we were together
As one

Parting Ways

I don't want to leave him
I don't want us to go our separate ways
I want to remain by his side
Now and forever more
I'm scared that once we part
He will forget our love
And find someone new
That all the promises we've made
Will be forgotten once again
I will miss being held in his arms,
The feel of his lips pressed to mine
I will miss knowing he's near
And always there for me
I don't want to leave him
I fear I'll never see him again
I don't know if my heart can take the pain
Of losing love once again

The Affair

It is a hard thing to do
Being in love with a married man
Your heart gets broken over and over again
And still you go back for more
You always hold onto the hope
That one day things will change
And all his promises will come true
Yet it is always the same old thing
Empty words and empty promises
Anything to get you to stay
He knows you will and you do
Because being with him
Even for just a little while
Is better than the alternative—
Sitting home alone with no one to call your own

The Voice

I picked up the phone
With trembling hands
And dialed the familiar number
I wanted to hear his
Voice, and find comfort
It rang three times
And a stranger said hello
My heart stopped
I couldn't speak
Where had he gone?
I discovered I'd never again
Hear the voice that
Brought me peace
It was gone forever
Tears welled in my eyes
It was beyond belief
He'd just been there
And now he was gone
Too suddenly for me to understand
And my heart broke
When it realized
The old, familiar voice
Would be no more

Going Home

As I sit here all alone,
I wonder when you'll take me home,

My life on earth seems useless and empty,
Even though I know you have kept me...

Kept me safe from this troubled world,
Where my thoughts of you are often blurred,

Because I struggle with my spiritual life,
It's filled each day with toil and strife;

I know all that I must do,
Is turn it all over to you;

You can help me with this strife,
And make me want to live this life...

Knowing that the time will come
When you'll look at my life in one lump sum...

Gaining or losing the rewards you'll give
To those who showed it was for you that they lived.

We've Had the Time of Our Life

Now we've had the time of our life
No, we've never felt like this before
Yes, we swear it's the truth
And we owe it all to you
'Cause we've had the time of our lives
And we owe it all to you
We've been driving for so long
Now we've finally found the road
To take us home
We saw the directions on the sign
As we left the Tennessee state line
Now with sunshine in our eyes
There's no way we could describe our
Destiny
So we took each other's plan
But we didn't understand
The urgency, just remember
This is one thing
We could get enough of
So we'll tell you something
We could be lost
We've had the time of our lives
No we've never felt like this before
Yes, we swear it's the truth
And we owe it all to you
With our body and soul
We wanted home more than you'll ever
Know
So we, just let it go
Weren't afraid to lose control

Yes, we know what's on our mind
When we say, "Stay on the road
Tonight," just remember
This is one thing we could get enough of
So we'll tell you something
We could be lost
'Cause we had the time of our life
And we've searched down every road
Till we found 441
And we owe it all to you
We've had the time of our lives
No, we've never felt like this before
Yes, we swear it's the truth
And we owe it all to you.

How Lucky I Am

How do I let you know
How lucky I am
To know you?
How lucky I am
To share my life with you
And a love like none
I've ever known before?
How do I let you know
How much your love
Has changed my life
And brought new meaning
To an otherwise lonely life?
I want you to know
All this and more
Because the love I feel for you
Is endless
A never-ending passion
And desire
To know you even more

Missing You

When you're not here beside me
I miss you more
Than words can say
There is an emptiness inside
That calls your name
A longing only your presence
Can take away
When you're not here beside me
I feel as if part of me
Is gone too
The part that knows
That by your side
Is where I belong
When you're not here beside me
I feel lost
In this ever changing world
Wondering if your love
Is real
Or nothing more than a dream
When you're not here beside me
I can't wait
Until we're together
Not just for that moment
But for now and forever

For My Love

When I think about you
I think about how much
Being with you has changed my life
How much happiness I feel
How much love I experience
How my soul cries out to you
Because you're the one
Who makes me whole
I never want to be without you
To feel the emptiness
Of a lonely heart
And the fear of knowing
There's no one special person
To share my life with
I love you, my love
With my whole heart
And pray each night
This feeling will never end

Two Hearts

I love you, Terry
With all my heart
There was a time
I thought I'd never love again
Then I met you
You helped me to see
That love is still possible
You helped me to believe
That love could flourish
When two lonely hearts meet
And become one
You brought new meaning to my life
And helped me to see
It was okay to love again

A Deep Longing

I feel your breath
Cool against my burning flesh
I feel your hands
Softly caressing me
And I burn with desire
I never want this moment to end
Yet I know it will
And you'll go home to her
My heart aches
From missing you
Wanting to be with you
Always and forever
Yet there's another I must compete with
A fight I don't want to wage
I just want you with me
Where you should be
Not with her
But with me
Now and forevermore

Forever Together

I want to feel his arms
Forever wrapped around me
I want to feel his lips
Forever pressed to mine
I want to know he's by my side
Forever, together, as one
I want to be his wife
Forever, walking by his side
I want this more than anything
Forever, together, our love no longer denied

What Is Love

What is love
But a fleeting thought
An emotion
That never comes to be
An idea
Planted in our minds
An emotion
We all feel
At one time or another
But one that rarely
Comes to be
An ideal we all choose
And long for
But rarely get to experience
A thought that we
Long to have
Yet it always leaves us longing
For something more

Tell Her Goodbye

I hate the thought of you with her
She's taken my place
And there's nothing I can do
But hope one day
That you'll be mine
Together forever
Until the end of time
For now I must take what I can get
And hope one day
Things will be different
When you'll be able to tell her goodbye
Because you feel the love
That has come into our lives

You're the One

I love you more than
Life itself
Without you near
I shed a tear
For you are the one
Who makes me whole
And you're the one
Who helped me see the sun
You brought to my life
A brand new day
And gave me more
Than words can say
I don't know what I'd do
Without you by my side
Keeping me sane
In a world where evil abides
You're my all
My everything
And there's nothing more
I could ask
Than to love you
With all my soul

My Heart Is Breaking

I wish I didn't have a heart
Because it is breaking all apart
With the thought of losing you
Because you've found someone new

Someone who fulfills your needs
Even though I begged you please
Not to go and run to her
For my pain there is no cure

I want you back in my life
To spend my life as your wife
Together forever as it should be
How can I get you to see

That with me is where you belong
A life with you is for what I long
To spend forever in your arms
To never again do any harm

To a heart that is full of love
Higher than that above
A love that will last forever and ever
And leave you alone never

Someone

I sometimes long for someone to hold
Someone to be there to make me feel whole

I long for a shoulder on which to cry
Someone to always be there and never say goodbye

I long for someone to share my dreams
Someone I can say is part of my team

I long to know if this person is there
The someone I can give my love and care

I long for the day when I will know
The someone who is the man my real self I can show

King of Kings

You shed your blood
To wash away my sin
Through your pain and suffering
I can begin again

You show your love every day
And I know you are always there
Doing all that you can
And listening to my every prayer

Help me to always remember these things
And worship you as the king of kings,
For no one can ever take away
All that you have given to me
Because, Lord, you are the king of kings

You've done so much for a fallen world
Where you are often only a blur
We get so caught up in day-to-day things
That our relationship with you is but a memory

When I do go astray
Leaving you out of my day
You get me back on the right of way
And show me how to go your way

Help me to always remember these things
And worship you as the king of kings,
For no one can ever take away
All that you have given to me
Because, Lord, you are the king of kings

A Special Love

I think of all that you gave to me
And everything through you I could see

My heart is filled with love
One so special it could only come from above

My love for you is oh so great
I can't wait to see you at the pearly gates

I want to please you the best I can
And know that because of you, I am

Your love is one no one can kill
And all you ask is I do your will

I give my life to one above
And remain forever filled with a special love

Letting Go

Letting go is hard to do
It means losing that special part of you

The part I have held very dear
And for which I have shed many a tear

But the time has come for me to say goodbye
And I promised myself I would not cry

And though the pain of it is great
I know for true love I must wait

And if waiting means having to let go
It also means as I person I will grow

Because letting go helps me to see
The special person I will one day be

Separate Lives

Sitting here thinking of you
My heart fills with a love I've never felt before
It reaches out to touch every part of my soul

By your side is where I long to be
To give you the encouragement you need
And the support we all desire

But here alone is where I am
Waiting for the day the Lord will bring
Two separate lives together as one

Did Jesus Shed Tears?

So many years ago
A baby boy was born
Right from the start
His presence was scorned
I wonder how he felt
Lying in the manager
Knowing all through his life
He'd face the wrath of others' anger

Did Jesus shed tears
While in the manager he lay
Was his heart full of fears
Of the price he would pay
Did he pray at this time,
"Father, not my will but thine"
Did Jesus shed tears
While in the manager he lay?

So many years ago
Through the desert he roamed
Fasting and praying
Knowing soon he'd be home
I wonder how he felt
Walking through the barren land
Feeling all of the pain
His life soon would be dealt

Did Jesus shed tears
While in the desert he roamed
Was his heart full of fears
Of the price he would pay

Did he pray at this time
"Father, not my will but thine"
Did Jesus shed tears
While in the desert he roamed?

So many years ago
In the garden he prayed
Down at his father's feet
His cup he did lay
I wonder how he felt
As he prayed there all alone
Feeling all the loneliness
He would claim as his own
Did Jesus shed tears
While in the garden he prayed
Was his heart full of fears
Of the price he would pay
Did he pray at this time
"Father, not my will but thine"
Did Jesus shed tears
While in the garden he prayed?

So many years ago
On a cross he was laid
Broken and beaten
The cost of our sins to pay
I wonder how he felt
As he hung there alone
Suffering in silence
So a greater love could be known

Did Jesus shed tears
While on the cross he did hang
Was his heart full of fear
Of the price he had paid
Did he still pray at this time
"Father, not my will but thine"
Did Jesus shed tears
While on the cross he did hang?

So many years ago
They laid him in a tomb
But death could not hold
This lovely bridegroom
I wonder how he felt
As he conquered the grave
Rising to his glory
And fulfilling the promise he made

Yes, Jesus shed tears
And each had a name
His purpose is clear
I am the reason he came
He prayed all the time
"Father, your will not mine"
Yes, Jesus shed tears
And each one had a name

My Special Friend

As I look over these past few months
It amazes me how our friendship developed;
We went from silence to sharing our deepest feeling.
When I look at what brought us together
I realize it was our mutual love of music
Through our music we shared our lives
Our good times as well as the painful ones.
Through our notes we learned about each other
And developed a bond like none I've ever known
The Lord has brought many special people into my life
Each one touching me in their own unique way.
You were no exception.
In you I see a reflection of myself
Both as I was and as I would like to be.
Though our time together has been short
And the time has come for us to part,
A bond has been built that will last forever.
For the Lord brought us together for a reason;
Though this reason we may not fully understand
I know in time we will be able to see
Why God chose this time to bring our paths together,
And created a friendship that will never end.
Thank you, my friend, for taking the time
To touch my life as no one has before.
Although our paths must once again divide
You will never be forgotten
And will remain someone special in my life

You and Me

From the first day I met you my heart was captured;
The gleam in your blue eyes
And the warmth of your smile
Made my heart beat a little faster

Very quickly our friendship blossomed
And we gave to each other a part of ourselves;
To me you gave warmth and attention,
To you I gave a heart in which love dwelled

The foolishness of other women gave me rejection
For in your heart dwelled pain and fear
Put there by those who failed to see
The tender part of you that was laid bare

Did I ever have a chance to win your love?
Or did the wounded heart refuse to see
That with the special parts I gave
Things could have been different for you and me?

The answers to these questions I will never know
But one thing will always remain true,
A part of my life you will always have,
And I will always remember you

For Bobby

Memories of you rush through my mind
Adding pain to an already wounded heart.
How can I remember the specialness of you
When each recalled word tears me apart?

I always held onto that small amount of hope
That one day you would feel for me as I did for you.
Now I know that day will never come
I have but one question, "What am I supposed to do?"

It is hard to believe you'll spend your life with another
She will fill the place in your life I longed to.
She will be the one to feel your warm embrace
She is not the one who means the most to you.

What am I supposed to do with this love?
Yours is being shared with another
Yet mine once again remains unfulfilled
Still longing to be shared with you and no other.

I know I must let go of a love I can not obtain
And by doing so lose another part of me.
Once again I have been unlucky in love
Because the true love I felt you failed to see.

You will always hold a special place in my heart
Because you touched my life in your own special way.
It is very hard to say goodbye
When every part of me wants to scream, "Stay."

I can not hold onto something that was never mine
Another dream will once again be denied.
As love once again betrays my trust
And the walls around my heart begin to rebuild.

The Visitor

He came while I was lost in dreams
With no consideration of me it seems

He came just as the day dawned bright
On the edges of a cold, dark night

He came much sooner than any expected
When he was least likely to be expected

DEATH!...
    He came knocking on my door...
BUT...it wasn't me he was looking for.
    HE came...
        To take...
            The one...
                I loved!

I Think

I think of you
I think of me
I see us together
I want this to be

I think of love
I think of forever
I see you leave
I want that never

I think of goodbye
I think of today
I see us apart
I want you to stay

I think of emptiness
I think of now
I see nothing
I cry deep down

I think of pain
I think of my heart
I see it in pieces
I cry for each part

I think of tomorrow
I think of new love
I see me with no one
I cry for lost love

Always

Always searching never knowing what each day will bring
Always trying to succeed never knowing when I will
Always striving to meet others' needs never knowing how mine will be
Always living in doubt and fear never knowing what to expect
Always hoping for the best never getting beyond the first step
Always fighting to survive never asking for a reason why
Always struggling to let other in never able to trust again
Always expected to be who I am never knowing exactly who that is
Always running from my secrets and pain never getting far enough away
Always wanting to be accepted never letting it happen
Always longing for love never opening my heart to receive it
Always looking at the negative never attempting to see the positive
Always wondering if I will make it through the day never letting the darkness completely
Take me in

Land of the Unforgiven

Living in the land of the unforgiven
Takes courage, strength and determination
For the war we fight is against ourselves
Though we try hard to find justification.

In the land of the unforgiven
Time stands still for the captives
For the victims come and go as they please
Without thought, care or concern for those who have adapted.

The land of the unforgiven is barren
There stands no tree of faith, hope nor peace
Each has been destroyed by anger, hate and greed
All waiting quietly for their day of release.

There is no joy in the land of the unforgiven
Only chains and shackles that wound and bind
A way of release seems far from being
For the transgressions of others are all that're on their minds.

The land of the unforgiven is a lonely place
Where rescuers are held at bay
Its captives desire to sit and brew
At least for one more day.

The land of the unforgiven can be destroyed
But only by those who created it
It will take will and humiliation
To bring you out of your self-dug pit.

Reality

Always running, living in fear
Of the realities that lie in wait
They hide in the darkness ready to pounce
Without regard for time, place or date.

Relief is not found in running
Nor in the bottom of a bottle, pot or crack
These only serve as a source of strength
For that which we try to attack.

We try endlessly to change the past
Rather than accepting it for what it is—
A part of us we can not forget
Something that forever lives.

Reality is not always as it seems
It can be good or bad
The difference comes in how we see
The experiences we have had.

The Battle

There's a constant battle deep within
The little me pushing for freedom
The big me holding it in, enjoying captivity
Slowly I begin to wonder who will win

Day after day the fight goes on
With neither side arising victorious
While one tries to mend and heal
The other reopens and rewounds

Am I the mediator of this war?
Will I be the one to decide just how long…
How long the battle will rage within
Allowing old wounds to be opened again and again

The War

Days like today are days, when memories of past hurts
Creep in and pray upon my mended heart.
Try as I might they won't go away
They insist on being reopened to bring this pain again
I try to control the raging battle and let healing emerge the victor
Sometimes hurts slip through the barrier
I have built and penetrate my weary soul
Other times I arise the victor and keep
The pain from overrunning my being and all I have become
I have learned that life is a constant battle
And wounds will be a part
So I will fight the best I can and accept the victories
As well as the defeats
For with every battle I gain new strength
And win more of the war.

Without and Within

Off in the distance, the sun rises to meet the sky
In my heart the clouds of despair rise to meet the rain
The sun is warm and bright, offering relief and solace
The clouds are dark and stormy, offering conflict and turmoil.

Off in the distance the ocean meets the horizon
In my heart the anger meets the bitterness
The ocean is calm and soothing, offering comfort and serenity
The anger is red with rage, offering confusion and doubt.

Off in the distance a bird soars high amid the clouds
In my heart the hurt soars high upon my soul
The bird is free and without concern, offering peace and tranquility
The hurt is bound and prisoner, offering fear and negativity.

In the distance a mother rushes to comfort her child
In my heart the loneliness rushes to tear me apart
The mother is loving and compassionate, offering care and concern
The loneliness is empty and painful, offering worthlessness and inadequacy.

Off in the distance peace brings healing
In my heart depression brings sadness
The peace is genuine and wanted, offering joy and serenity
The depression is cold and hungry, offering death and reckless abandon.

Off in the distance I am presented with a choice
In my heart I know there is but one answer
The choice is hard and requires much, offering change and contentment
The heart is unsure and afraid, offering nothing that will forever remain.

You

Have you ever watched a sunset,
And how its beauty radiates across the whole night sky?
Have you ever stood and looked at the ocean
And how it seems to span across the whole earth?
Have you ever looked deep within yourself
And seen how much of yourself you confine?
Like a sunset, our inner beauty should radiate everywhere.
Like the ocean, we should reach out to all the earth.
Yet, like a crab we cower away from the outside world
We stay in our shells and only appear when we are alone.
The presence of others makes us cower in fear
Or bite and snap in anger and bitterness.
Why do we fear that to which we are called?
What will it take to draw us out?
What will it take for us to become the person we are to be?
The answer lies in the sunset.
The answer lies in the ocean.
The answer lies within our shell.
Look deep within and you will see
That what it takes to be you, is you.

Questions or Comments?
The author would love to hear from you.
You can contact her at:

Misty J. Grimes
P.O. Box 2014
Hardwick, GA 31034
mjgrimes@alltel.net

Printed in the United States
64412LVS00002B/43-45